_____

A gift for

_____

From

Tiny Tidings of Joy

for You,
Dad

Illustrations by Jeannie Mooney

Published by J. Countryman, a division of Thomas Nelson, Inc.,
Nashville, Tennessee 37214

Project Editor: Terri Gibbs

Designed by Left Coast Design Inc., Portland, Oregon

ISBN: 08499-9669-4

www.jcountryman.com

Printed in Singapore

A tiny tiding
of good cheer:
"I'm glad you're my dad,
every day of the year!"

Let it snow!
  Let it snow!
    Let it snow!

When the snow
falls gleaming white
And the stars
shine oh so bright,
Let the bells ring
loud and clear,
Christmas time
is here!

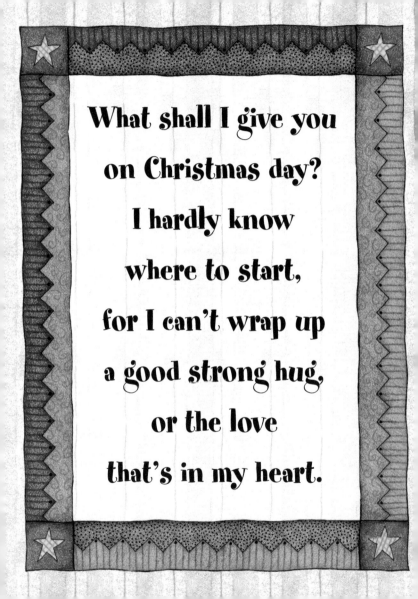

What shall I give you
on Christmas day?
I hardly know
where to start,
for I can't wrap up
a good strong hug,
or the love
that's in my heart.

Candy canes

of white

and red . . .

the fresh-baked smells
of gingerbread,
Christmas is
the time of year
when friends
and family
gather near.

Some of the reasons why
I think you're the best, Dad:

_____

_____

_____

_____

_____

My dad is the best!!

_____

_____

_____

Dad knows best... because he is the best!!

Once upon a time ... a candy maker created the perfect candy to symbolize the true meaning of Christmas. It was the candy cane. The white stripes would stand for the purity of Christ and his Virgin birth. The red stripes would signify the pain & death Jesus endured on our behalf. The hook shape would also be a reminder to all people of the name Jesus & his role as Good Shepherd.

May your heart
feel the joy
and welcome
the love that
God sent down
from heaven
above.

Hearts go home

at Christmas.

**Join hands
and hearts
across the miles,
give away
laughter and
lots of smiles.**

Blessed be
the LORD your God
who has
delighted in you.

1 Kings 10:9

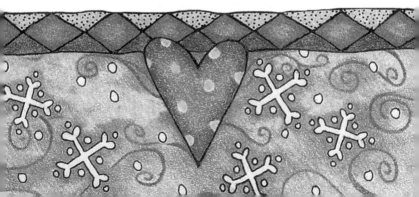

**Stockings hanging
by the tree ...**

**love shines down
on you and me.**

If I could fill your stocking with any gift in the world, I'd fill it with:

Twinkling stars glowing bright,

sleigh bells in the snow,
smiling faces by firelight,
it's Christmas wherever you go!

Love amazing...

Love divine.

The star
shone bright
on Christmas
night,
a note of love
from God above.

Wishing you a Christmas day that is blessed in every way.